1,000,000 Books

are available to read at

---◆---

www.ForgottenBooks.com

---◆---

**Read online
Download PDF
Purchase in print**

ISBN 978-1-5282-2704-9
PIBN 10897357

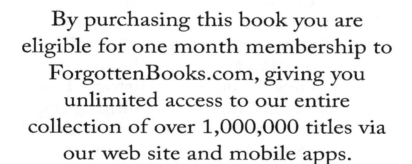

Conservationist

Published by the Department of Wildlife and Fisheries in the interest of conservation of Louisiana natural resources.

the Louisiana Department of Wildlife and Fisheries (LDWF).

This 2,000-acre lake was lowered to its floor in 1986 so that a new spillway structure could be constructed on its northeastern end.

Taking advantage of this drawdown, the LDWF chose Chicot Lake to begin an intensive Florida bass stocking program, beginning with the release of 800 subadult Florida bass (10 inches long) into Chicot Lake's new waters in December of 1987. Since that time, Florida fingerlings were added on an annual basis for a sum total of 600,000 Florida bass stocked in these waters since 1987.

Considering the numbers of bass released and Chicot's small size, it came as no surprise that an increase in bass density was experienced by anglers -- despite a catch-and-release requirement.

The ultimate goal of the LDWF is to increase the size and catch rate of the largemouth population of Lake Chicot, and an initial management paradigm included a 10-fish daily creel with a minimum length limit of 14 inches. This was done so that the LDWF professionals could track the 1988 year class (1988 spawn and fingerlings released) of these fish and make further adjustments.

In January of 1990 a more restrictive creel of five bass with a length limit of 16 inches was imposed to add further protection to that year's class. Finally, in the spring of 1991, Chicot Lake became classified as a "Quality Lake" in accordance with the "Louisiana Black Bass Fishery Management Plan" designed by the LDWF.

Since that time, and eight-fish daily creel with an associated 14-17 slot limit has been enforced as the 1988 year class moved within these parameters. Only four fish above 17 inches are allowed in the creel.

For those unfamiliar with slot limits, it would be legal to take a combination of eight bass 14 inches or less and 17 inches or more in length. However, only four of the bass can be above 17 inches.

Regarding angling opportunities at Chicot, Coldiron had experienced some fantastic numbers during the spring spawn of 1990. On one guiding trip with a couple of New Orleans anglers, over 200 bass were taken on one day with a "keeper" rate of five percent.

"It was as tremendous, memorable trip,"

Photo by Chris Berzas

LDWF's efforts to turn Chicot Lake into a true "quality" bass fishing lake have included a complete drawdown, restocking with Florida strain bass, careful monitoring and strict regulation.

Photo by Chris Berzas

indeed possible by using this method. However, if it's extremely cold, your best bet may
be to use a jigging spoon and fish the curves
and bends of the main channel.

The spawn appears to correspond with the
onset of February, when increased numbers
of bass can be taken in comparison to January.

Coldiron suggests that visiting anglers fish
the Branch Cove area and other coves between the Branch and south landing on the
western side of the lake.

"It's not uncommon for bass to move up in
a foot of water in these areas," remarked
Coldiron. "They can be found near the cypress
trees, brush piles and sunken timber that
clutter this midwestern section."

Coldiron suggests that the bass angler come
equipped with spinnerbaits and crawworms
as the baits of choice. He prefers half-ounce
Bulldog spinnerbaits in solid chartreuse or a
blue/white chartreuse combination with a
gold #4 or #5 willow-leaf blade.

During the peak of the spawn (late February and March), Coldiron recommends fishing the banks within the coves that hold a lot
of cypress trees. Working the spinnerbait at
about 18 inches of depth has proven to be a
noteworthy pattern at this time.

Topwater lures are also effective, especially in the early morning. Sluggos, gold
Rattlin' Rogues, Tiny Torpedoes and buzzbaits
are good choices.

Regarding the size of Chicot largemouths,
a few surprises were noted beginning in 1988
when Coldiron's friend Bobby Ortego caught
the first keeper of their trips -- a 3 1/2-pound
bass that measured more than 17 inches.

During the spawn of 1990, Coldiron landed
a five-pound bass that was identified as a pure
Florida fish -- possibly one of the subadults
released in 1987.

Other anglers caught hefty largemouths in
1989 and 1990, ranging from 6 pounds 12
ounces to 7 pounds 10 ounces.

A real shockwave came when LDWF gill
net samples taken in 1989 revealed three hefty
largemouths weighing 5.3, 6.5 and 8.3 pounds.

**Visiting anglers to
Chicot Lake should
fish the Branch Cove
area and other coves
between the Branch
and south landing on
the western side of
the lake.**

reminisced Coldiron, "although only a very
few fish were keepers. In the spawn of 1991,
the numbers were not so exaggerated. Yet on
a good day, you could catch 45 to 50 fish. An
excellent day produced 60 to 75 bass."

Coldiron maintains that the early part of
the year can be real slow. "Most of the fish can
be taken in the Branch Cove area, in six to eight
feet of water on points and near the base of
cypress trees," he said.

Coldiron recommends flipping a Bulldog
jig 'n' crawworm combination around the base
of cypress trees, working this bait very me-
ticulously to catch the attention of a wintering
bass with a low metabolism. Limits of bass are

The largest fish, which was apparently stressed and later succumbed, proved to be a rapid growing, initially stocked subadult approximately three years old.

LDWF gill net samples resumed in 1990 and resulted in two fish in the nine-pound range and other hefty six and seven-pound specimens.

In 1991, lunker interest exploded at Chicot when a Lafayette angler harvested a 9.2-pound largemouth. In the summer of '91, an Oakdale resident caught a 10.5-pound lunker.

Although the size of these fish has Louisiana anglers quite excited, the 13-pound bass recorded at Lake D'Arbonne and Caney Lake overshadowed Chicot Lake largemouths in terms of weight.

However, the improved catch rate of quality largemouths is an additional advantage that serious bassophiles seek in the fertile waters of the Bayou State. The only comparisons of increased bass density to date are the early days of Toledo Bend, and the tidal bass action experienced in brackish water marshes.

Hopefully, angler compliance with current length restrictions and future management practices will transfer the current experience of "numbers" at Chicot Lake to future encounters with noteworthy, wallhanging lunkers.

Chicot Lake is located within beautiful Chicot State Park some six miles north of Ville Platte on La. Highway 3042. Once entrance is gained for a $2 per vehicle fee, anglers will find two landings that access the lake -- one each in the north and south sections. The south landing is adjacent to the park's first entrance off 3042 and provides a relatively large launching area.

This highly rated state park offers such amenities as 27 fully equipped cabins, two large group cabins, over 100 RV spurs and an Olympic-sized pool usually open between June 1 and Labor Day.

For more information regarding maps, camping reservations or other concerns, write to: Chicot State Park, Route 3, Box 494, Ville Platte, LA 70586, or call (318) 363-2403. □

Photo by Chris Berzas

Photo by Guy LaBranche

Mining Golden Eggs From Choupique

BY HOWARD ARCENEAUX

Until a few years ago, bowfin got little respect. That has changed, thanks to some enterprising entrepreneurs who found a use for this plentiful fish. Caviar, made from bowfin roe, is used by some of Louisiana's most renowned chefs in five-star restaurants.

hen opportunity knocked at Ray Carline's door in December of 1986 he reluctantly answered it. Opportunity, it turned out, was disguised as a stocky, bespectacled LSU pre-law major named John Burke.

Carline, a third-generation commercial fisherman from Charenton, extended his right hand to Burke. It was scarred with deep lines and callouses hardened by a lifetime spent fishing the waters of the Atchafalaya Basin. Little did they know this meeting was about to change their futures and their fortunes.

Burke explained the purpose of his visit. He wanted to sample something called "choupique caviar."

For at least four generations a caviar recipe had been passed down through the Carline family. Carline and his three brothers figure it was brought over by their ancestors from Italy.

Choupique, also known as bowfin, has long had an undeserved reputation. Fishermen discard this ancient fish from their nets and consider it a nuisance. Carline knew choupique was good for something. Burke wanted in on the secret.

Bowfin are distant cousins of sturgeon, paddlefish and garfish. Their roe makes excellent caviar, except for garfish, which are not used for consumption.

Caviar has become a symbol of wealth in American culture. Hence the paradox with bowfin. The Rodney Dangerfield of Louisiana's fish produces a highly sought-after food served at five-star restaurants and mansions of the rich and famous. The meat is as popular as road kill.

Until World War I, the United States produced so much caviar from the cold waters of the

Atlantic Ocean it was exported to the Soviet Union. Caviar was so cheap, American saloons freely offered it to their patrons like contemporary pubs hand out bowls of pretzels. Thirsty customers have always made bar owners happy. Today the choicest and most expensive caviar comes from the Caspian Sea area. Russian and Iranian caviar are made from the roe of beluga, the largest member of the sturgeon family. However, decimation of breeding habitat, overfishing and pollution have contributed to declining beluga numbers. The war between Iran and Iraq during the 1980s further hampered beluga harvesters.

The price skyrocketed. Distributors in the United States turned to less expensive domestic sources of roe.

Paddlefish and American sturgeon were an attractive alternative, but their limited numbers could not support pressure from commercial demand. Eggs from other fish are also used to make caviar. For instance, red caviar is made from salmon roe while golden caviar comes from whitefish. Lumpfish roe is dyed black or red. But nothing commands the respect, nor price, of naturally black caviar.

When processed properly, the bowfin roe turns black and has a distinctive texture and taste. When Burke sampled Carline's caviar, his immediate impression was that it looked and tasted like the real thing.

"Where do we go from here? How much of this can you make?" Burke asked Carline. He said he could do a few thousand pounds pretty easily.

The optimum time to harvest bowfin eggs is just prior to spawning, from the first part of December through late February. Carline produced the first batch and Burke began searching for distributors and markets for "Cajun Caviar."

He sold 500 pounds to a Texas caviar wholesale broker and other sizable quantities to importers in New York. They said it was excellent "filler" for the more expensive variety made from sturgeon roe. If bowfin caviar could be used as filler, Burke reasoned, it could also be promoted as genuine stuff.

Burke eventually changed the focus of his education and in his spare time, he continued to get his fledgling company off the ground. He and Carline incorporated the Louisiana Caviar Company in 1989, renamed the product Choupiquet Royale and got it and the name "Cajun Caviar" federally trademarked.

Burke started peddling his new product to different chefs around Louisiana. Most were impressed with the caviar's quality. They were equally astounded that it came from bowfin.

John Folse of Lafitte's Landing near Donaldsonville was among the first chefs to recognize the value of Choupiquet Royale. Others, at Commander's Palace and The Upperline in New Orleans and Juban's in Baton Rouge, soon followed.

William Boyd, executive chef and food and beverage director at Branberry's in Baton Rouge, uses Burke's caviar to garnish his dishes. In fact, Boyd used the caviar with a sauteed crawfish dish that won a gold medal in seafood and Best of Show at the 1989 Culinary Classics of Baton Rouge. He also won a gold medal at the 1990 Culinary Classics for an oyster entry using bowfin caviar. Last September, at the Gulf Coast National Seafood competition, Boyd won first place in seafood with a crabmeat with caviar custard, beating out 30 other teams of chefs from across the nation.

"Once I got it into those types of white table restaurants, the business started snowballing," said Burke. "I have been trying to expand to other markets and we have had a lot of interest from people overseas."

Choupiquet Royale currently has customers in Beverly Hills, Tokyo and Melbourne, Australia. Burke has also been negotiating with wholesalers in Europe. Burke estimates he sold 3,000 pounds of caviar last year and hopes to increase production to 5,000 pounds in 1992.

"I think it's an expanding industry,' Burke said. "Caviar has been here since Aristotle's

Biologists monitor bowfin populations, taking samples with gill nets.

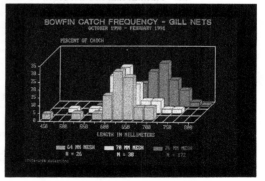

BOWFIN CATCH FREQUENCY - GILL NETS
OCTOBER 1990 - FEBRUARY 1991

Photo by Guy LaBranche

**Randy Montegut
gently spoons finished
bowfin caviar into
Imperial Orleans tins at
his processing plant in
New Iberia.**

time so for caviar to go away during the next hundred years is not likely. As long as we have a good quality product, and the demand for it, I think the industry will be here and continue to grow."

Choupiquet Royale is not the only Louisiana-produced bowfin caviar on the commercial market. Randy Montegut, a former biologist with LSU Sea Grant, started Bon Creole in New Iberia about a decade ago as a crawfish processing plant. Looking for something to produce in the offseason, Montegut developed his own brand of bowfin caviar. He got the idea from Burke.

After much trial-and-error experimentation with recipes, he began selling it two years ago under the name Imperial Orleans. Montegut's company sold more than 1,500 pounds of caviar last year and he expects to surpass that total this year. The bulk of his sales are to Louisiana customers although he hopes to expand to other domestic and overseas markets.

"I would like to produce as much as I can and have it under my own label," said Montegut. "The amount of bowfin caviar being produced is not a lot. We have to get people out there to realize the product is on the market."

Montegut is reluctant to reveal much about his caviar production operation. He is supplied bowfin roe mainly from Atchafalaya Basin fishermen, although some comes from other areas.

Burke is supplied with bowfin by a limited number of commercial fishermen in the Charenton area, many of whom Carline has known his whole life. Large gill nets are used to harvest the bowfin and the live fish are delivered for processing. The fresher the caviar, the better. The caviar needs about a week to reach its peak.

Burke calls his finished product "Malossal" caviar, a Russian adjective meaning "lightly salted." Neither Imperial Orleans nor Choupiquet Royale contain artificial coloring or preservatives. Under optimum conditions, bowfin caviar has a shelf life of six months.

Coloring and cod liver oil are added to Russian caviar to extend its shelf life. Iranian caviar, once a staple in this country, has been banned since the late 1970s by the Federal Food and Drug Administration because boric acid is used as a preservative.

"The competition is tough," Burke said. "There's not that many people into caviar and it's not easy to make a good quality caviar

from choupique roe. Our actual process is a trade secret and if you try to apply some other recipe to choupique eggs, it just doesn't work the same."

The retail price of Choupiquet Royale is around $10 an ounce, a bargain considering beluga caviar goes for $75 an ounce. However, Montegut would not reveal what he charges. He and Burke intentionally keep their prices below other types of domestic and imported caviar.

"The best caviar is not the one which costs the most, it's which one you like the most," Burke said. "It's a matter of educating the American caviar-eating public. If you like one that costs $75 an ounce, that's the one for your taste."

Bowfin remains an underutilized species. Once the eggs are removed, the carcasses are given back to the fishermen who sell the meat or use them as food for pond crawfish.

Burke would like to change what he considers a waste of good fish. He has been seeking ways to market bowfin meat and has experimented with smoking it, and with making boullettes (seasoned balls similar to hush puppies). He has also considered making inexpensive fish patties that could be sold to Louisiana's correctional facilities and educational institutions.

The Louisiana Wildlife and Fisheries Commission last year established a statewide 22-inch minimum size limit on bowfin harvested for commercial purposes. Another regulation prohibits commercial fishermen, while on the water, from possessing bowfin eggs that are not naturally connected to the whole fish.

LDWF biologists have been conducting growth and population studies on bowfin and want to make sure these plentiful fish do not suffer the same fate as paddlefish.

In November of 1989, the LDWF closed the harvesting of paddlefish, commonly known as spoonbill catfish, for an indefinite period.

In certain parts of the state, the low number was due to the slaughter of paddlefish for their roe by fishermen. It's unlikely the statewide bowfin population will be seriously affected by the current commercial roe demand. On the other hand, species management is needed to protect it from depletion.

Perhaps an article by influential Los Angeles Times food writer Rose Dosti best summed up the potential of bowfin caviar. She included Choupiquet Royale on her list of "in" dishes for the 1990s. "If you can find it," she wrote. □

ELLOW THUNDER-

ELPING BOX TO SIX MONTHS

gundog, guard dog and most importantly, a loving, affectionate pet. In other words, a year-round dog, not one we would hunt waterfowl with for two months and then ban to a kennel.

Plus, we decided not to use force methods during training -- no ear pinching or electric collars. Our goal was to develop a dog that would, out of desire to please, do the same tasks as dogs trained using force methods.

You will experience what we did — searching, picking the pup, training and the first hunt. Our adventures will appear in three articles during the year. We will share our mistakes but also our joys and successes with bonding Mellow Thunder, our new retriever.

Success in the field with a retriever begins long before any hunting trips. The process starts with the search and selection of the pup. Being aware of what to look for can prove to be valuable later on.

Photo by Carle E. Dunn

Retrievers are curious about ducks from an early age, in both controlled and natural enviroments.

Photo by Carle E. Dunn

SEARCHING

If, like us, you don't know critical details about retrievers, the purchase decision is major. This dog would be our daily companion for over a decade. We read books. We found two of the best to be *Training the Hunting Retriever* by Jerome B. Robinson and *Retriever Puppy Training—The Right Start For Hunting* by Loveland and Rutherford.

Robinson is gundog editor of *Sports Afield* magazine. His book contains training techniques related to him by professionals. More importantly, his work concentrates on developing a gundog that uses its natural hunting instincts. Some gundogs receive training that takes the wag from their tails, the gleam from their eyes and the affection from their hearts. They become mechanical dogs.

We learned that black labs were loving,

affectionate animals. Females, in particular, can be most loving. We have grandchildren and wanted a family dog; thus, we decided to get a female. This choice caused difficulties that we'll later explain.

THE WHELPING BOX

A whelp is a newborn pup. A whelping box is used by the mother to bear and oversee her young. The box has an open side for the mother to exit and enter. This opening must have a lower edge that is high enough that pups cannot exit. The pups' eyes are not open and they could wander into harm's way.

If possible, arrange to observe pups while they are in the whelping box. This helps in the purchase decision. You will learn how the breeder cares for the dogs and can observe individual traits. However, quality retriever pups are usually sold before birth. There is a priority selection system of who gets a particular pup. We were well down the choice ladder- -last!

PICKING OUR PUP

We talked to friends with labs and to the United Kennel Club, UKC. We received recommendations to buy from a professional breeder. The advice was to select a dog with a good genetic background and with parents proven in the field. According to Bob West, professional trainer and advisor for Ralston Purina, a sound genetic background is the foundation of a good retriever. Coming from proven parents enhances the likelihood of getting a dog with known potential. Developing this potential comes through training.

After checking references, we selected a professional breeder with a litter due. We had also checked the backgrounds of the sire and dame. Both were field proven and had excellent genetic backgrounds. Furthermore, a breeder will provide documentation to prove this. Documentation consists of registration papers. Registration can be with the American Kennel Club (AKC), UKC or both. Require the breeder to provide an Orthopedic Foundation for Animals (OFA) number. This reduces the possibility of serious hip ailments later. Don't buy if the breeder does not produce the papers.

Check with your veterinarian. He will advise you about required immunizations. Have the breeder provide the pup's immunization record. Be wary of any breeder who does not provide records that vaccinations are complete. If he won't, don't buy the dog.

Loveland and Rutherford recommend getting a pup when it is six or seven weeks old. This is a most amenable bonding time. Bonding is when the pup establishes relationships with creatures in its new home. Bonding does not have to be solely with humans. We later learned bonding takes strange routes.

I examined the pups' living conditions for cleanliness. I observed their feeding. In particular, I looked for pot bellies and skinny bodies. This is a sign of worms. Watch reactions. Are they lively and full of energy? Do they frolic and play or are they slow and nonresponsive? Look for limps or peculiar gaits while moving. A clean, shiny coat is a sign of good health.

Having only two pups from which to choose, I took each to an area to be alone. One lay in my arms without moving or reacting, while the other licked my face and was a bundle of energy. The lethargic pup, when placed on the ground, would not move. When I walked away, it would not follow. Upon being called with clapping hands, it curled in a ball. It did not move.

The other one followed when I walked. It chased when I ran. Upon stopping, it leaped into my arms and commenced washing my face. These were good signs.

I examined their bodies from tail tip to nose. I was looking for reactions to touch such as jerks or pain indications. The slow dog seemed to have a reaction upon touching its left rear leg. Also, it displayed a slight limp when walking. This could be nothing more than a minor sprain from playing. Yet, I never saw it attempt to play.

Look for fluid from eyes and a runny nose. Check for fever. Ask for a thermometer to check temperature. Normal is 101.5 degrees. Beware of the breeder who will not provide a thermometer. Reputable ones always have them available.

We would like to think that we selected Thunder, the energetic pup, but, we're sure she selected us. Time reinforced this belief.

We stopped at our veterinarian's office. He examined Thunder. While his physical examination found nothing awry, he noted that Thunder's immunizations were incomplete. The doctor administered them. I had disregarded previous advice.

Many myths disappeared in following months. Until a pup reaches six months, let it be a puppy! Of course, there are necessary things such as toilet training, basic obedience and socialization.

Toilet training was the easiest. Correction of two mistakes did the chore. I took Thunder to the soiled area. Rolling her on her back by gripping loose skin at the neck, I stared into her eyes. This put Thunder in a submission position. A gentle head shaking and a resounding "No! No! No!" worked. I took her outside each time. Afterward, she either went to the door and cried or came to me and did the same. At night, usually around 2 a.m., she nudged me or Jean from bed.

"No" becomes an important word in obedience training. Yet, in one case, it had little meaning to Thunder: chewing furniture. Thunder could chew a foot-thick table leg into pieces. After rubbing many recommended concoctions on furniture, bed clothing and so forth, my patience was at an end. She kept chewing.

An idea came from watching the movie "Cool Hand Luke." Paul Newman evaded bloodhounds by spreading pepper during a jail escape. I mixed red pepper with water in a used, hand-pump, spray detergent bottle. It only took one application. One taste and Thunder's gnawing ended. We supplied her with old shoes and leather dog bones. She confined chewing to these.

Socialization is important during the first six months. We took Thunder everywhere we went. She met dogs, adults and children, and encountered different situations. She gained experience, and some restraint, though she kept her enthusiastic, loving nature. Whenever she became a nuisance, we simply tethered her with a leash. She lay down and went to sleep.

We started fetch training too early at four months. We succumbed to bragging by others of how early their dogs passed field trials. Little did we know that many of them used electric collars and forceful methods to do this.

The next article will reveal how we learned to gain Thunder's hunting obedience through training and fun. We'll also tell of some major goofs and their effects on Thunder. □

Bonding and socialization of a puppy are most important during the first six months.

FISH

FOR THE

Future:

THE ROLE OF FISHERIES MANAGEMENT PLANS

**BY JOHN ROUSSEL
AND HARRY BLANCHET**

There has been a recent proliferation of "fishery management plans," or "FMPs," for a multitude of marine and freshwater species in Louisiana and the Gulf of Mexico. These plans often bring on harvest restrictions, including closed seasons, new size and bag limits, and quotas on commercial harvest. In some cases, as in the red drum (redfish) fishery in federal waters, whole segments of the fishery have been closed on a semi-permanent basis.

What are these "plans"? Where did they come from, and why are they needed?

Let's keep in mind that some of Louisiana's fisheries, such as shrimp and oysters, have been under management for many years. Only recently, though, have there been efforts to develop comprehensive, documented fishery management plans (FMPs) for fisheries in our state and adjacent offshore waters.

Documented plans were virtually non-existent for fisheries in the United States until the 1980s. It was not until passage of the Magnuson Fishery Conservation and Management Act of 1976 that comprehensive documents began to be developed for fisheries in the federal waters.

At first glance, it may seem hard to understand how natural resources as valuable as our fisheries did not demand formal management plans until recently. The fact that fisheries, especially marine fisheries, were viewed as being limitless, and the fact that fisheries are common property resources, have tended to discourage comprehensive approaches to management.

In addition, the effects of excessive exploitation on fishes are less visible than these same effects on land animals. Until recently, there were few documented cases of complete collapse or of recovery under management. Some fish stocks have persisted under heavy sustained fishery pressure for nearly a century. Other fisheries, such as the California sardine fishery, have collapsed primarily due to factors other than overfishing, including changes in ocean current patterns, and physical or chemical environments.

Recently, though, the list of fish stocks which are considered overfished has been rapidly growing and the thought of fish stocks as being limitless is now recognized as myth.

But what is overfishing? In reality, many things may be called overfishing. Generally speaking, though, two types of overfishing are recognized. The first, and most dramatic, is recruitment overfishing. This occurs when the stock is fished so heavily that the remaining adults do not have the capacity to replace the harvest. The most obvious example of this was the overharvest of the great whales by modern whaling fleets. The other more common form of overfishing is growth overfishing. This occurs when fishing pressure reduces the size of the average fish caught to the point that the yield of the fishery is reduced.

Yield is normally expressed as the biomass (weight) harvestable in a fishery, but the actual yield may be expressed in other terms as well. In a trophy fishery where yield is expressed in terms of the number of trophy-sized specimens that may be harvested, maximum yield of trophies may be far less weight than the maximum yield of total biomass the fishery could provide.

In the early years of development of FMPs, much of the money for the development of these plans went to examining fisheries in the Northeast and Northwest U.S., while fisheries of the Gulf of Mexico received relatively little attention. This situation has changed and we are now seeing the result of this increased attention.

To understand the true role of exploitation (fishing) we must realize this is only one factor affecting fish populations. Other factors, including habitat quality and environmental conditions, influence the numbers of fish available to fishermen.

Many species important in Gulf of Mexico fisheries are estuarine dependent. They require certain types of habitat in the marshes, bays and bayous of our coast to sustain healthy population levels. These habitats are now undergoing extreme changes that have not been seen before in this area. The effects on species dependent upon these habitats can only be estimated.

The type of management required for a given species is very dependent on the life cycle of the species. For this reason, most good FMPs include an extensive section on the biology of the fish. Warm water, estuarine-dependent, fast-growing species of the Gulf of Mexico require different strategies than cool-water, continental shelf-dwelling, slow-growing species of more northern latitudes. Even within our area, species such as shrimp, oysters and crabs, which spawn as one-year-olds with prolific reproductive ability, need to be considered differently from longer-lived animals with lower reproductive abilities, such as sharks (see article in Sept./Oct. 1991 *Louisiana Conservationist*).

One of the most difficult and important points of fishery management is the concept of "common property." This alone could be the subject of many articles, but the basic idea is fairly simple: The fish belong to everyone equally so, unfortunately, it is to the advantage of fishermen in any fishery to harvest fish before anyone else gets them.

The fish are equally available to all, so if one fisherman leaves while there are still fish to

Large nets are used to gather fish in coastal marshes, bays and bayous for sampling.

LDWF file photo

LDWF file photo

Electrical shock machines are utilized by biologists to collect fish for population sample purposes.

LDWF file photo

catch, another fisherman can catch these, and the first fisherman loses that portion of the available catch.

This almost always leads to overfishing because as the fish become more scarce the price received by commercial fishermen has often increased.

Recreational benefits are not measured by price, but may also increase since increased harvest often increases desirability.

These increases may end up encouraging the harvest of more just at the time when harvest should be restricted, not expanded.

Any management system, be it fishery management or otherwise, involves a sequence of steps from the definition of problems and objectives to the execution of remedial action.

Successful management of fisheries is a complex process which includes a mixture of biology, economics, sociology, law and the decision and management sciences. It also involves a large number of participants. A sound fishery management plan provides an organized approach to intelligent and proper management by ensuring that all available information and the pertinent law and decision-making framework are presented.

A management process must go through a series of steps to optimize results. In the development of FMPs, a series of seven steps is, at least in theory, the basis for the procedure. These are:

1) *Define objectives* There is seldom a single objective in any management program. One of the objectives is always to prevent overfishing so that a continued harvest is possible. Beyond this, objectives of the FMP are very dependent on the species involved. There may be a desire to maximize harvestable biomass (total weight) of the species, increase average size of fish harvested, or to increase opportunities for harvesting "trophy" fish.

2) *Collect data* Some data necessary to make decisions may already be available, but other data may require research before a complete answer can be had for some questions. It may not be necessary to delay the FMP process until all data is collected, but the initial FMP should identify

areas where data collections are needed.

3) *Extract and verify information* Information from varied sources, collected for different reasons and with a variety of perspectives and applications, must be put into a form that can be used to analyze and understand the species.

4) *Build decision models* Decision models help describe various options available to managers for the fishery. Inputs may include information on the recreational and commercial fishery, age or size structure of the fish stock, and biological data on the species.

5) *List options and formulate action plans* These describe potential benefits and costs of each option in standard terms. One problem in comparing shared fisheries, where different user groups are fishing the same stock, is that it is often difficult to determine benefits and costs to society as a whole. Costs and benefits for one segment of the fishery might be more or less offset by effects on other segments.

For spotted seatrout, for instance, increasing the recreational size limit would eventually allow some fishermen to harvest a larger average-sized fish, but would reduce the average number of fish taken by all anglers. It might especially affect some anglers, such as beach/bank fishermen and winter fishermen who historically harvest a smaller average size of fish and who may not have a boat to have access to larger fish.

6) *Implement decisions* Once the options are listed and evaluated, some will be implemented.

One option which should always be considered is the "no action' option. In some cases, this is most appropriate. If not, some regulation of the fishery will be changed. This may involve changes in seasons, size limits, quotas, gear regulation, etc. Changes may increase or, more commonly these days, decrease harvest.

Before implementing regulations, some form of public notice is given by the agency involved unless it is an "emergency action." Modifications to original proposals often result from this process.

For instance, if the species is regulated by a state legislature, the notice is done by filing bills, which may then be modified during the legislative process before becoming law.

If the species is regulated by a state or federal conservation agency, some sort of comment period is generally required, after which public comments and agency responses are evaluated by an overview authority such as the Office of Management and Budget at the federal level, or the Legislative Oversight Committee in Louisiana.

7) *Evaluate decisions* Once the rules are set, monitoring of the stock is required to see if the species responds to the change in fishing pressure and if responses are similar to the changes predicted. If not, re-evaluation of all the previous steps is required.

Even if the changes are similar to predictions, this may be due only to coincidence of strong year class strength at the time the regulations went into effect. A well-designed, long-term monitoring program is necessary to distinguish between these possibilities.

One factor that will inevitably influence the number and detail of the FMPs for an area is the monetary and manpower resources dedicated to the task of researching and managing fisheries.

That is "what" a fishery management plan is, but the "why" is equally important.

In the Gulf of Mexico, and throughout the oceans of the world, increasing fishing pressure and more sophisticated and effective fishing techniques necessitate monitoring and sound management.

Sound and effective management, however, requires more than a few dollars.

In Louisiana, landings data indicate that commercial fisheries have a dockside value of about $250-$350 million per year. The value of recreational fisheries is less well documented, but a study by the U.S. Fish and Wildlife Service suggests that expenditures by recreational fishermen are in the neighborhood of $600 million. To manage these resources, the Department of Wildlife and Fisheries will spend about $3.5 million this year for marine monitoring, research, data collection, analysis and management.

It is simply not enough. By comparison, one private marine lab in Florida spends as much each year for marine research alone!

Although FMPs are never popular with everyone, and are sometimes popular with no one, ever-increasing exploitation of our offshore, near-shore and inland fisheries, coupled with man-made and natural habitat degradation, has made professional management of fisheries imperative.

Fisheries are renewable in perpetuity, but unless society demands and funds the necessary habitat protection and management programs the future of our fisheries could be far from bright. □

Editor's Note: *A licensed fisherman in Louisiana can keep five redfish and 25 speckled trout. That's the total possession limit as well as the bag limit. Only two cobia can be bagged, and two king mackerel and three amberjack. There are also size limits to obey.*

These and other bag and size limits have been bitter medicine for many Pelican State anglers accustomed to "catch all you can and keep 'em all" fishing.

The fact is, fisheries are finite and exhaustible resources. Dramatically increased fishing pressure by the commercial and recreational sectors in recent years dictates that these resources be managed responsibly.

This article was prepared by professional fisheries biologists in the Marine Fisheries Division of the Department of Wildlife and Fisheries.

LDWF file photo

From hardwood bottoms to upland forests, Pelican State hunters are matching wits with wily birds this spring.

Sportsmen are seeking male turkeys - called gobblers. Once allegedly proposed by Benjamin Franklin to be the United States' national bird, this keen-eyed gallinaceous (ground nesting) feathered creature is elusive and difficult to bag. Still, this species, *Meleagris gallopavo*, has a weakness -- spring romance. Successful hunters know how to make music for romantic gobblers.

A turkey hen's melodious clucking attracts gobblers. Yet, the tonal quality must be precise and the presentation correct. Many of today's hunters use commercial calls in an attempt to entice birds within range of their weapons.

Still, there was a time when hunters had to use homemade calls as commercial varieties were not available. Moreover, there are those who make and use such devices today. Often, this craft passes from generation to generation and takes many forms.

John Gentry, of Many, La., is not unlike Antonio Stradivari. Stradivari made violins during the early 1700s. Using trial and error, he worked with materials to hand-produce violins of exacting tonal quality. His sons learned from him.

Gentry makes turkey calls and, like Stradivari, his sons learned his craft. The walls of John's home hold trophies of three previous state record turkeys besides many others. Each succumbed to a precise tone and use of handcrafted turkey calls.

John became interested in turkeys during the 1960s. He worked for Louisiana's Department of Wildlife and Fisheries' Game Division. He helped trap and transplant birds across the state. Subsequently, he became manager of the Sabine Wildlife Management Area near his Many home. He retired in 1987.

During this time, he saw his first wild turkeys. "We were trapping turkeys," he said, "and moving them to other suitable habitat in Louisiana. I became interested in the birds and their habits. I developed a desire to make turkey calls."

There are three typical homemade calls. One is the box, which is rectangular and hand size with a paddle-like device attached. The paddle is called a striker. The user moves the striker across the top edges producing a chirp-like sound. Another is the slate. Originals consisted of jagged pieces of slate sized to fit

Photo by Carie E. Dunn

into one's palm. The user rubbed a dowel-like rod of pencil size across its surface to produce sound. Tone quality varies from a sound similar to scratching fingernails on a blackboard to that of a receptive hen. With slate difficult to get, some makers use plexiglass as an alternative.

The third is a wing-bone. As the name implies, this call is crafted from the bone of a turkey's wing. Gentry speculated, "This call was likely used by colonists. Indians used calls and I suspect they learned from them."

The former game manager began his quest to build calls. His sons Joe, Gary, Keith and Gregg were at home. Joe, Gary and Keith became enthralled and began to build and experiment. John Gentry credits his sons with most of the successes. Not only did they work hard at developing calls, they used them in the field to bag birds. Joe, in particular, was excellent at harvesting trophies. Their handcrafted calls played a major role.

BOX CALLS

Gentry explained that the first call he ever saw was a box call. It was made from a cedar fence post and a piece of persimmon wood. The box was cedar and the striker persimmon. "In those days folks used local materials. They didn't have an opportunity to obtain different woods from across the country."

According to John, old-timers had different ideas about wood types to use. Each produced a different tone. Yet, two driving factors were available wood and ease of use. Joe explained, "A certain locale may have an ample supply of Bois de Arc. This is one of the most dense woods in North America. It grows in southeastern Louisiana bottoms and bears a pod that looks like an apple. I made a box call from one but do not like it because it is too hard."

Cedar and ash are distributed throughout Louisiana and both woods have excellent tone qualities. Construction plays a significant role in producing box calls. "The sides of the box are probably most important. The upper edges, where the striker touches, need sanding that changes tone. In addition, thickness plays a part. Tone varies with thickness," Joe explained.

Trying to get a sound conducive to luring a gobbler within range requires the user to know the most enticing tone to produce. "Learning this is simple. All a person needs to do is to go where someone raises turkeys and

listen," John added.

In use, the Gentrys coat the boxes' upper edges with chalk or pine rosin powder. Joe prefers pine rosin because, while hunting, there may be rain. "The pine rosin stays dry while rain washes off chalk powder. If this happens, the box edges get wet and lose their ability to produce proper tone," he said.

While having seduced gobblers with melodies from each call type, the Gentrys prefer boxes. "Turkeys are wary birds. Their eyesight is keen. If an approaching gobbler spots movement, it's gone," Joe said. "I can place a box next to my leg while sitting against a tree and operate it with one hand and minimum movement. This lessens chances of a spooked bird."

SLATE CALLS

"Slate in its natural state," John explained, "is difficult to find in Louisiana. The boys located an old school being demolished and got pieces of blackboard to use.' The consensus among the Gentrys was that slate makes an excellent call. Yet, it has disadvantages. First, a hunter usually must use both hands which creates too much movement. Plus, if slate gets wet, it's useless as a call.

Folks have cut plexiglass and sanded it as a substitute. The Gentrys use a striker with a plexiglass tip to enhance sound. The striker is similar to a pencil with a rounded end.

WING BONE CALLS

Considered by some the oldest of calls, the Gentrys use a bone from the upper half of a turkey wing. There are two in the upper part. They use the smaller of the two.

"Old-timers," John said, "cut the ends off and hollowed the bone. They blew into it or sucked on it to produce hen sounds. Some folks are really good at it."

Joe said there are bone calls on the market that are not bone but plastic. While they're bone colored, they are not true bone. Plus, he said he has removed the refill portion of ballpoint pens and used them as turkey calls. "Gobblers came to the sound," he said.

Despite what homemade call a person chooses to use, an essential ingredient is practice. According to the Gentrys, the process requires patience, tuning and a constant effort to produce a tone that gobblers recognize as a hen — nothing less will do. So, if you're going gobbler romancing this spring, be prepared to play the right song. □

Three effective ways to attract romantic turkeys are with box calls, slate calls and wingbone calls.

Homemade calls require patience, tuning and a constant effort to produce a tone that gobblers recognize as a hen.

Photo by Gregg Gentry

LOUISIANA'S
artificial reef
PROGRAM
BY RICK KASPRZAK

guidelines to establish well-developed, well-organized artificial reef programs. In 1985, some Louisiana citizens became concerned about the required removal of offshore oil and gas structures and loss of important reef habitat and associated fishing opportunities. They formed the Louisiana Artificial Reef Initiative (LARI). LARI was a unique blend of state, federal and university representatives, members of various recreational and commercial fishing interests, and representatives of Louisiana's oil and gas industry. Modeling state legislation after NFEA, LARI members developed the Louisiana Fishing Enhancement Act (LFEA), or Act 100, to provide the authority to develop a comprehensive artificial reef program for Louisiana. Signed into law on June 25, 1986, Act 100 established Louisiana's Artificial Reef Development Program and named and outlined the duties of three participating agencies. This program was given the responsibility for siting, maintaining and enhancing artificial reefs in both state and federal waters off the Louisiana coast, utilizing but not limited to retired oil and gas structures.

The program is administered by the Louisiana Department of Wildlife and Fisheries (LDWF) with the staff of Louisiana State University's Center for Wetland Resources' Coastal Fisheries Institute and Louisiana Geo-

More than 680 platforms had been removed as of 1990 with an estimated 2,000 platforms expected to end their primary lives as oil and gas structures by the year 2000.

Photo by Rick Kasprzak

A Rig at South Timballer 128 is pulled on its side as it becomes an artificial reef.

criteria for siting artificial reefs in Louisiana's waters. The Louisiana Artificial Reef Plan was drafted in 1987 and approved by the Senate and House Natural Resources Committee in October.

After a lengthy process to identify areas where reef development was inappropriate, such as shipping lanes, pipeline corridors and bottoms traditionally used by the commercial fishing industry, as well as existing live bottoms, public hearings were held across south Louisiana to outline the program and select areas where reefs should be located. As a result of those hearings, nine artificial reef planning areas were selected where specific artificial reef projects could be sited during the first phase of the program. The establishment of the nine planning areas facilitates planning by the oil and gas industry in determining abandonment schedules for offshore facilities, thereby encouraging industry cooperation.

The Louisiana Artificial Reef Trust Fund was also created by Louisiana's Fishing Enhancement Act to run the program because no monies were allocated from the state's general fund. These funds are supplied by participating operators donating half the savings realized over a traditional onshore abandonment of structures. The donations are deposited into the legislatively protected trust fund and the

program is run off the interest generated by that fund. It has been estimated that the oil and gas industry can save approximately $1 million or more per structure, depending on water depth, by converting its obsolete structures into artificial reefs as opposed to the traditional onshore abandonment.

Operational expenses for the program include, but are not limited to, program administration, monitoring of reef sites to insure permit compliance and document reef performance as well as buoy purchase and maintenance for the artificial reefs to provide safety of navigation and enable fishermen to locate them. As the interest exceeds operational expenses, other activities such as reef-related research and the construction of inshore artificial reefs can be funded.

Since the Louisiana Artificial Reef Program was approved in 1987, six sites using the underwater support structures (platform jackets) from 16 obsolete petroleum platforms have been established. Participating operators include Chevron, Oxy (formerly Cities Service), Exxon, CNG, Mobil, Mesa, Unocal and Odeco and Kirby. Kerr-McGee and Shell are making plans and negotiating with the state to donate structures this year.

Offshore oil and gas operators continue to be interested in participating in the Louisiana

Artificial Reef Program. Negotiations to obtain platforms and associated monetary donations are done on a case-by-case basis between the operator of the platform and LDWF. Size, location, distance from shore, water depth, resale value, and proximity to a reef planning area are some of the factors which affect the cost of converting a platform into an artificial reef. It is not always economically feasible to convert every platform into an artificial reef.

Current Coast Guard regulations also dictate where these structures can be sited. The Coast Guard requires a minimum of 50 feet of clearance over the top of the reef, buoying the reefs with the less expensive, more easily maintained, unlit reef markers. This limits the water depth where many of the reefs can be located. In many cases the reefs need to be sited in a minimum of 100 feet of water.

The Louisiana Artificial Reef Program is currently investigating and establishing guidelines for the creation of artificial reefs in Louisiana's state and inshore waters. The first priority is to identify obstructions in Louisiana's coastal waters which are already acting as de facto reefs. Over 6,000 wellheads, shellpads and platforms have been identified and their locations mapped. Identifying and evaluating these obstructions is necessary to determine their effectiveness as reef materials and to decide whether to enhance some or all of these reefs with additional materials. Plans by the LDWF are under way to produce a series of maps identifying these locations for public use. These fishing maps are expected to be available to the public by the beginning of the summer for a nominal fee.

Thus far, two shellpad reefs have been constructed off Redfish and Cypremort points in Vermilion Bay utilizing funds generated by the offshore program. In addition, two others are slated for Terrebonne and Timbalier bays for the spring of 1992.

Federal and state governments, the oil and gas industry, as well as Louisiana's fishermen have already benefited from the state-supported artificial reef program. Continued cooperation of all the groups involved and support of the Gulf user groups insures that Louisiana's program will enjoy success in the future.

EDITOR'S NOTE: For more information on Louisiana's Artificial Reef Program contact Rick Kasprzak at P.O. Box 98000, Baton Rouge, LA 70898. □

It takes less than three minutes for a rig to sink to the bottom.

Photo by Rick Kasprzak

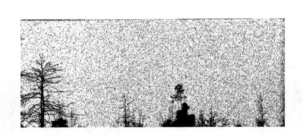

BY MAURICE COCKERHAM

West Bay Wildlife Management Area holds the distinction of being the oldest WMA in Louisiana. It was first established in 1948 through an agreement with the Wildlife and Fisheries Commission and a private timber company. At present, West Bay has grown to encompass more than 55,000 acres.

The entire area is owned by Boise Cascade, Louisiana Pacific and Quatre Parish timber companies and made available to the Department of Wildlife and Fisheries without charge. Long term agreements were renewed in early 1991 - which assured the continued availability of West Bay WMA well into the next century.

West Bay WMA is located in north-central Allen Parish. It is accessible on the north from state highways 10 and 112, and on the south from state highway 26.

The terrain is generally flat, with about one third of the area comprised of a poorly drained "bay gall." The remainder is fairly well drained. Mill Creek, on the southern end of the area, is the only significant waterway and is classified as "semi-flowing."

Forest cover ranges from small pure hardwood stands to sprawling pure pine plantations composed of loblolly and/or slash pine.

The lush, generally thick understory type, varies with the timber variety. Common species are youpon, rattan, arrowwood, smilax, blackberry, dewberry, huckleberry and varied annual legumes and grasses.

The relatively dense understory provides excellent food and cover for species such as deer, squirrels and woodcock. In the more open areas quail and doves are readily available.

The predominant understory type also provides an excellent rabbit population, and a season was recently established to allow hunting the cottontails and swamp rabbits with beagles. This particular activity has proved to be very popular and quite successful.

Deer populations on West Bay are good, providing excellent hunting opportunities, and some impressive trophy bucks are taken on the area each season.

For the past three years, a special "youth hunt" has been conducted on the area by the Department of Wildlife and Fisheries, with many youngsters succeeding in harvesting their first deer. Regulations for the special

WEST BAY GAME MANAGEMENT AREA

hunt, and other activities, are contained in the department's annual hunting and fishing pamphlets.

Other activities available at West Bay include bird watching, hiking, berry picking, nature study and photography, and trail riding.

The nearby town of Elizabeth sponsors a "Christmas in the Country" festival in December of each year. About 1000 riders converge on the Wolf Bay camping area on the west side of the area, off La. 112, and utilize designated roads. There are more than 300 miles of unimproved roads on the area for organized and individual horseback rides. ☐

West Bay WMA's relatively dense understory provides excellent food and cover for species such as deer, rabbits, squirrels and woodcock.

The Best Buys of the year...

The *Louisiana Conservationist* magazine and *The Official Louisiana Wild Game Cookbook* are guaranteed to keep your interest all year long.

Don't delay. The magazine costs $8 for one year, $14 for two years and $24 for four years. The cookbook is only $14.95. Order now!

A CLOSER LOOK

omnivores. Omnivores such as raccoons, bears and humans, eat both plants and animals to survive. Carnivores eat only meat and have well-known adaptations such as their sharp teeth and claws, and their ability to stalk and

PREY

By Lyle Soniat and
Eleanor Abrams
Louisiana Sea Grant College Program

Most people watch with uneasy fascination as a cat stalks a mouse, or on television, as a shark glides past in search of prey. These images reveal a side of nature that may seem cruel, but many animals must kill for nourishment. Plants, by photosynthesis, are one of the few organisms that can combine free flowing energy such as the sun with nutrients in the soil to sustain life. The animal kingdom has evolved to take advantage of this concentrated energy and nutrients stored within plants and within other animals.

Within the animal kingdom, herbivores, or plant eaters, evolved first. By consuming part or all of a plant, herbivores can use the energy in plants to move, maintain their bodies, grow and reproduce. The nutrients help to build and to repair parts of the body such as muscles, skin and organs. Like all animals, herbivores need a steady supply of both energy and nutrients to survive.

With the evolution of herbivores, animals called predators evolved to eat them. There are two types of predators: carnivores and

blood to a wounded fish. If predators are so efficient, why do you suppose they haven't eaten all the prey animals?

First of all, prey animals are not completely defenseless, but they have physical adaptations to escape or avoid capture such as camouflage coloration to escape detection. Rabbits, for example, are brown and blend into the dead leaves on the forest floor. In the north, the rabbits' coat turns white in the winter and matches the snow on the ground. Secondly, avoiding a predator can be just as important as not being seen. In some species, eyes are located on the side of the head to allow for maximum viewing of their surroundings. A predator's eyes are often located in the front of its face. While predators don't have as wide a viewing capability, frontal vision allows them to focus on prey when attacking. Compare, for example, the placement of the eyes in pictures of a deer and a cat.

In addition, prey animals have also developed a wide variety of behavioral adaptations when threatened with attack by predators. For example, bats emit a high-pitched squeak to help locate their prey, the moth. As the squeak bounces off the moth, the bat can detect differences in the sound and this helps it locate the moth in the air. However, some species of moths can hear the squeaks and will stop flying to drop several feet in the air to escape being captured by the bat. Similarly, rabbits remain motionless to avoid detection in the presence of a predator.

The very young, the old, the weak, the injured and the sick are often the animals most predators can easily capture and eat. When these animals are removed from the population, the remaining population has a better chance of survival by having less competition for food, water, cover and space. This also greatly increases the vigor of the population and allows a much higher reproduction potential because the animals are much healthier.

There is a dynamic balance between the predator population and the prey population. All animals produce more offspring than the

If predators are so efficient, why do you suppose they haven't eaten all the prey animals?

The very young, the old, the weak, the injured and the sick are often the animals most predators can easily capture and eat.

PREDATOR/PREY

*Resource
managers
recognize the
importance of
predators'
roles in
maintaining
the balance of
the ecosystem.*

land can support, and there is a surplus of prey and predators annually. The predators live on that excess. If the prey animals have an especially good breeding year because of improved habitat conditions, the population of prey animals will increase. This in turn allows the predator population to build because it too has plenty to eat. So as the prey population grows, so does the predator population. However, if the prey population has a bad breeding year, for whatever reason, there are fewer young produced. It will now be harder for predators to obtain food and they or their young could starve. The number of predators in an ecosystem is tied directly to the existing number of prey that it feeds on, usually following the same population trends of either building up or decreasing in numbers a year later than the prey species.

No predator, except man, has the capacity to totally exterminate a prey population. Fortunately, it is also within man's power to restore animal population through sound resource management. Until about 50 years ago, many predators were killed at every opportunity, and some predator populations were eliminated from their traditional habitats. Red wolves and panthers, which formerly roamed the woods of Louisiana, were hunted to extinction in the state. They were unable to adapt to their changing environment and man. Man did not understand the need for predators, blaming them for killing game animals and destroying his livestock. Besides taking only a small percentage of annual reproduction that would die anyway, many predators are beneficial to man. Owls, hawks and snakes eat rats and mice, thus reducing crop damage. One barn owl alone is capable of killing as many as 8,000 rodents annually.

Resource managers now recognize the importance of predators' roles in maintaining the balance of the ecosystem. Predators are now managed, either by protection or harvesting, to maintain a healthy breeding population. Even with our new perspective about the need for predators in an ecosystem, some predators cannot be reintroduced into areas where they once existed. The large unbroken habitats needed to support large predators do not exist any longer. Man's need to develop land for homes and agriculture has cleared away great tracts of forest land. The remaining land left is critical for the support and survival of these predators and their prey.

AMERICAN Swallow-tailed Kite

BY JIM ALLEN AND WAYNE NORLING

Marked among its kind by no ordinary beauty of form and brilliancy of color, the kite courses through the air with a grace and buoyancy it would be vain to rival." These words, written in 1874 by ornithologist Elliot Coues, describe as well as any the American swallow-tailed kite (*Elanoides forficatus*). Coues wrote about the kites he saw in North Dakota and other northern states, where the species was once fairly common. Today, however, the kite is essentially a bird of the Deep South. The American swallow-tailed kite's breeding range has undergone one of the most dramatic declines of any North American bird of prey and Louisiana is one of only six states that apparently still supports a breeding population. Nobody knows exactly what caused the decline.

It is estimated that only 860 to 1,010 pairs are left in the entire United States. The vast majority of these are found in Florida, but as many as 150 pairs may exist in Louisiana and Mississippi.

In addition to its beauty, grace and rarity, there are many other reasons why this species is so interesting. One especially appealing characteristic of the kite is its gregarious nature. It is not unusual to see kites traveling or foraging together in small groups.

One especially appealing characteristic of the kite is its gregarious nature. It is not unusual to see kites traveling or foraging together in small groups.

Pre - 1880

1940 - Present

Louisiana is one of only six states that apparently still supports a breeding population of kites. Nobody knows exactly what caused the decline of this once abundant bird.

appear to be "birds of leisure." Small groups occasionally perch together in a large tree until as late as 8 or 9 in the morning, long after most birds have started going about their business. Most likely, they are waiting for thermals to develop, since they tend to glide more than most raptors. Also, much of their prey becomes more active once the sun has been up for a while.

What may be most intriguing about the kite, however, is just how little we actually know about its status in this state. It appears certain that kites breed in Louisiana, but no record of a nest has ever been published. Occasionally, individuals that appear to be immatures are sighted and once, on April 25, 1957, a lone kite was seen carrying a twig, possibly indicating it was building or repairing a nest. That is the entire extent of evidence that a breeding population does indeed exist!

Reports from other states indicate that nests are most likely to be found in large pines in or close to large swamps adjacent to rivers. The only nest reported in Mississippi was also found in a large pine in the vicinity of Van Cleave. Nests have been found in other types of trees, such as bald cypress, but most nests found outside of southern Florida (where kites often nest in mangroves) have been in pines.

We know almost nothing about population trends of kites in Louisiana and no statewide survey has ever been conducted. A few observations are reported every year, which seem to indicate that a small, stable population exists, but we simply cannot be sure of the kite's status without regular surveys.

If you would like to see American swallow-tailed kites, the most likely places to find them are in the northwestern part of the Atchafalaya Basin and in the lower Pearl River basin. Occasionally, kites have been seen in the New Orleans vicinity and as far north as the Ouachita Wildlife Management Area near Monroe.

Any sighting of a nest or a group larger than 30 individuals would be well worth reporting. Places to report your observations include the authors at the U.S. Fish and Wildlife Service, National Wetlands Research Center, 1010 Gause Blvd., Slidell, LA 70458, (504) 646-7304; Jennifer Coulson, c/o Louisiana Science and Nature Center, 11000 Lake Forest Blvd., New Orleans, LA 70127-2816, (504) 246-5672; or Bill Vermillion, Louisiana Department of Wildlife and Fisheries, P.O. Box 98000, Baton Rouge, LA 70898-9000, (504)765-2976.   □

The largest groups reported in Louisiana number 20 to 30 individuals, but groups of several hundred have been seen in Florida. Large groups are seen most often when the kites first arrive in late March or early April, and again after nesting season, from early July until they leave in late August or early September.

Another interesting and impressive characteristic of kites is the apparent ease with which they manage to capture and eat prey in flight. The kite's diet consists largely of insects, small reptiles and amphibians, although they have also been reported to take an occasional small bird, mouse or bat. Kites even drink on the wing, skimming low over a lake or stream and scooping up water with their bills.

At times, American swallow-tailed kites

LAW LINES

Behind the Badge
BY CAPT. KEITH LaCAZE

Turkey Hunting Regulations

Louisiana's 1992 Turkey Hunting Season will begin with the March 21 opening of Area B in the southeastern portion of the state. Area A follows on March 28 and Area D on April 11. Area C, which includes portions of Ouachita and Richland parishes is closed this year. Preseason reports indicate good turkey populations throughout the state and hunters can expect to find gobblers in quantity.

The regulations pertaining to turkey hunting have no new changes or restrictions. We should, however, review existing regulations and discuss safety. Baiting laws are of particular concern and will be explained in detail.

The license requirements for turkey hunting are a basic and a big game hunting license for residents of age 16 to 59. Visitors from out-of-state, age 16 and older, are required to have nonresident licenses. The limit is one gobbler per day with a season limit of three. Still hunting is the only legal method and the use of dogs, baiting, electronic calling devices and live decoys is prohibited.

Legal firearms for turkey hunting are shotguns, including muzzleloaders. Shot may be no larger than #2 lead or BB steel shot. They may also be taken with bow and arrow but by no other means. No rifles of any caliber may be used. Some states allow the hunting of turkeys with a rifle, but Louisiana does not.

Hunting over bait is the most common violation wildlife agents encounter during the spring turkey season. Title 56, Section 124 (10) (a) of Louisiana

Laws Pertaining to Wildlife and Fisheries states:

"No person shall hunt, trap or take turkey by the aid of baiting or on or over any baited area." The subsection defines baiting as "The placing, exposing, depositing, distributing or scattering of shelled, shucked or unshucked corn, wheat or other grain, salt or other feed so as to constitute for such birds a lure, attraction or enticement to, on or over any areas where hunters are attempting to take them." An area is considered baited during the time the feed or salt is present and for 15 days after complete removal of all feed or salt.

The regulation does not prohibit "The taking of turkey, on or over standing crops, grain crops properly shucked on the field where grown, or grains found scattered solely as the result of normal agriculture planting or harvesting." Neither does it prohibit the taking of turkey where grain, feed or salt has been distributed or scattered as the result of "Bona fide agricultural operations or procedures, or as a result of manipulation of a crop or other feed on the land where grown for wildlife management purposes; provided, however, that manipulation for wildlife management purposes does not include the distributing or scattering of grain or other feed once it has been removed from or stored on the field where grown."

Essentially, this regulation prohibits hunting over grain or feed which has been brought to an area and distributed for the purpose of hunting turkeys. It does not prohibit hunting over wildlife food plots or grain fields.

For law enforcement purposes a person is considered to be hunting over bait if he is calling, concealed or positioned within 100 yards of a baited site. The baited site is only that immediate area where bait is deposited.

If you intend to hunt an area it is a good idea, if at all possible, to check thoroughly for bait prior to the hunt. It is not uncommon for an unsuspecting hunter to be within 100 yards of a baited site without being aware of its presence. Walk through the area and check particularly those locations where you find scratching or other evidence that turkeys are feeding. Also, be obser-

vant of other wildlife. Numerous birds flying to and from a site may indicate bait. Anyone who finds a baited area should report it immediately to a wildlife agent.

Every experienced hunter knows that turkey hunting, one of the most exciting forms of hunting, is also the most dangerous. Each year throughout the country hunters accidentally shoot other hunters during the turkey season. These accidental shootings often result in serious injury and even death.

Protect yourself by wearing hunter orange while walking to and from your hunting site. Hunter Safety experts also recommend carrying decoys and harvested birds in blaze orange bags. A band of orange cloth around a tree near your blind is another good idea.

In a situation where another hunter is approaching your position, let him know you are there by speaking to him. Movement such as waving or standing up may cause him to fire. Using your voice is much safer.

Hunting fairly and reporting violations are the responsibilities of the turkey hunter. This, combined with aggressive restocking efforts and effective enforcement, has resulted in expanding populations of this great game bird throughout the state. Continued support and protection will insure that the wild turkey gobbler will "sound off" on spring mornings for generations to come. □

Photo by Capt. Keith LaCaze

Conservation

Notes

Memorial Fund Established to Honor Wildlife Agent

A memorial fund has been established to honor Wildlife Agent Ricky Dodge, who died in an accident Jan. 20.

Col. Winton Vidrine, chief of LDWF's Enforcement Division, reported Agent Dodge was killed when his four-wheel all-terrain vehicle overturned while he was attempting to cross a ditch.

The accident took place near Mansura while Agent Dodge was investigation a closed-season hunting complaint. He was struck in the head when the vehicle fell on him.

Agent Dodge, 37, was a 12-year veteran of the Enforcement Division and at the time of his death was a member of the statewide Special Task Force. He is survived by his wife and two children. Contributions to the fund may be addressed to the First Pentcostal Church, 99 Benjamin Dr., Marksville, LA 71351, Attn: Rev. T. Michael Crist.

Two Legislators Honored for Role in Duck Stamp Program

The Louisiana Wildlife and Fisheries Commission honored Rep. Francis C. Thompson of Delhi and Sen. William E. Crain of Rayville at its January meeting for their role in establishing the state's Duck Stamp program.

The two lawmakers served as lead authors of the bill that enacted the stamp during the 1988 legislative session. Thompson, an ardent sportsman, told the commission and its audience that he considers the Louisiana Duck Stamp bill perhaps the most important legislation he has sponsored in his 18 years in the legislature.

Stamps and prints sold to hunters and collectors brought in $1.4 million in 1989-90 which is the most money ever generated by a first-of-state Duck Stamp program. Monies derived from the program go to provide a stable funding source for the acquisition and protection of Louisiana's valuable wetlands.

Spring Elected Operation Game Thief President

Dr. David A. Spring, a Baton Rouge podiatrist and hunting enthusiast, has been elected president of Operation Game Thief, Louisiana's grass roots anti-poaching campaign.

Spring succeeds Charles E. Wiggins Sr., who was elected treasurer at OGT's annual meeting in January. Other officers elected were Robert Dugal of New Iberia, vice president, and Colt James of Alexandria, secretary.

Named as directors were W.H. Chapman (Lake Charles), Vincent Darby (Arnaudville), Edwin Delancy (Shreveport), Nookie Diez (Thibodaux), Dr. George Dugal (Lafayette), Marc Dupuy Jr. (Marksville), Felix Horaist Jr. (Sunset), Larry Rabalais (Innis) and Susan Wiggins (Shreveport).

In 1991, OGT paid out $9,500 in rewards in 41 cases of lawbreaking. Since the program's inception in mid-

1984, OGT has paid out $76,000 in rewards. As its goal for 1992, the volunteer organization is seeking to establish an endowment fund with major corporations as contributors. Interest from the fund would be used for rewards.

National Wildlife Week April 19-25

The National Wildlife Federation and its state affiliates have chosen "Endangered Species: We're All in This Together" as the theme of the 1992 National Wildlife Week. During the week of April 19-25, people of all ages will participate in this annual celebration.

In addition, April has again been designated as Earth Action Month to emphasize the importance of people taking action to protect the environment.

To help the country celebrate Wildlife Week, the NWF and its state affiliates will distribute more than 600,000 education kits, free of charge, to educators across the country. Included in the kits are a 16-page educator's guide, a theme poster, a 12-picture poster, a sheet of wildlife stamps, an educational materials flyer and a sheet describing an opportunity to win a scholarship to Wildlife Camp.

Hummingbird Booklet Published

The Louisiana Department of Wildlife and Fisheries' Natural Heritage Program has published a new booklet entitled *Louisiana's Hummingbirds* by Nancy L. Newfield. The booklet contains various information on hummingbirds such as their life cycles, proper feeder maintenance and plants for attracting these birds.

The booklet also includes illustrations and photos of hummingbirds found in the state. *Louisiana's Hummingbirds* can be obtained free from the LDWF. The address is: Louisiana Department of Wildlife and Fisheries, Library, P.O. Box 98000, Baton Rouge, LA 70898-9000.

Lifetime Licenses Holders

Effective Jan. 1, 1992, the Louisiana Department of Wildlife and Fisheries began to offer Lifetime Hunting, Fishing and combination licenses to residents and nonresidents. The Lifetime Licenses, available for a one-time fee, encompass all recreational privileges currently covered by the basic licenses.

So far, 17 Louisiana residents have purchased the Lifetime Licenses:

Serrhel Adams	Baton Rouge
Mark Berggren	Marrero
Steve Brinson	Columbia
Travis Brinson	Columbia
Paul Collins	Ruston
Kenneth Dorris	Livingston
Landon Farrell	Slidell
Johnny Gemar	Jonesville
Eric Hayes	Lafayette
Dakota Jones	Lake Charles
Jason Newschurch	Port Allen
Frederick Parent	Chalmette
Emile Rainold	New Orleans
James Rawls	Bastrop
John Rhodes	St. Joseph
Timothy Ritchie	Harvey
Jeff Schneider	Ponchatoula

Law Enforcement Graduates 25 Cadets

Twenty-five cadets graduated from the Louisiana Wildlife and Fisheries Law Enforcement Training Academy in mid-February. The cadets, who made up the academy's third class, will be assigned to districts throughout the state and will significantly increase the number of LDWF field agents.

An academy consists of 21 weeks of intensive training in wildlife law enforcement. Among the areas studied are hunter safety, boating safety, ATV and boat operation, first aid, defensive tactics, firearms, compass navigation and DWI detection.

Those graduating were Rayford Aucoin, John Becker, Stuart Boykin, Michael Brown, James Carter, Michael Drude, David Folse, James Garon, Damian Grossie, Darren Guidry, Craig Hidalgo, Herbert Hinton, Steven Lucia, Jubal Marceaux, Scott Matthews, Shawn McRae, Todd Moreau, Peter Oliver, Bart Robichaux, David Snell, Bruce Spillers, John Tarver, Jimmy Vining, William Vosbein and Patrick Wiley.

Commercial Fishermen Get New Style License

The Louisiana Department of Wildlife and Fisheries has discontinued the traditional paper commercial fisherman's license and replaced it with a new commercial fisherman's sales card.

The new sales card, which resembles a credit card, is embossed with the commercial fisherman's name, license number, Social Security number, expiration date of card and residency status.

The card is presented by commercial fishermen to wholesale/retail dealers at the time of a sale. It verifies the seller possesses a valid fishing license and allows dealers to record the pertinent information for their records.

Louisiana Sportsmen's Show in Superdome

The 13th annual Louisiana Sportsmen's Show and Sale is scheduled for March 11-15 at the Superdome in New Orleans.

Among this year's features are fishing tackle and boats, hunting outfitters and equipment, outdoor travel and wildlife art. There will also be continuous seminars with national fishing and hunting celebrities.

Survey Reveals Hunter Ethics as Important as Safety

A majority of hunter education coordinators believe classes should emphasize good hunter ethics as much as safety, according to a year-long national survey conducted by the Izaak Walton League of America.

Deer were listed as the game species most often associated with illegal or unethical hunting practices by 97 percent of the respondents.

Louisiana Black Bears Listed as Threatened Species

The U.S. Fish and Wildlife Service has listed the Louisiana black bear as a threatened species, granting the animal official protection under the Endangered Species Act. The listing is based primarily upon the loss of and continued threat to the bear's habitat, according to service officials.

Threatened status means the bear is likely to become endangered within the foreseeable future throughout all or a significant part of its range. The black bear, once found extensively throughout Louisiana, southern Mississippi and parts of eastern Texas has had its habitat reduced by more than 80 percent with encroaching civilization. The animals exist in Louisiana today primarily in the Tensas and Atchafalaya River basins.

LDWF file photo

No More Goose Creeping Could Lead to Ban on Squirrel Hunkering

FUNNY SIDE UP

BY GLYNN HARRIS

Artwork by David Norwood

If you hunt waterfowl in Louisiana, you are no doubt aware that "goose creeping" is against the law. And well it should be. While I wholeheartedly agree that it is unsporting to crawl a quarter mile on your belly to get to blast at a bunch of sitting geese, I can't help but be a bit concerned.

The thing that worries me is that the powers-that-be might decide one day to outlaw "squirrel hunkering."

At the risk of sounding smug, I must admit that I'm a pretty fair squirrel hunkerer. In the unlikely event that there is a reader out there who is unfamiliar with the how-to's of squirrel hunkering, I'll explain. (The rest of you may skip the next few paragraphs. I already anticipate your comment..."not another story on squirrel hunkering. I'm as tired of reading about this as I am about a major kitchen appliance playing tackle for the Chicago Bears.")

Okay, fella, it's just you and me. Pay attention now and I'll tell you all you need to know about squirrel hunkering.

It's best to employ this technique when hunting in tandem with a partner. The two of you are sneaking through the woods when a squirrel spots you and scoots upstairs to hide among the leafy branches. Hopeless? Nah...not if you're adept at squirrel hunkering.

If it's your turn to shoot, your partner walks noisily underneath the tree where the squirrel is hiding and continues on through the woods, singing some raucous Cajun drink-ing tune until he is well out of sight. "I'm Just NUTS About You, Cher" seems to work well with squirrels.

The acorn-sized brain of the squirrel fires into action about this time, putting thoughts into the rodent's head such as, "Duh, they're gone, so it's safe to come out now." While squirrels may be adept at solving complex trigonometry problems, it is a well-known fact that they can't count. Two of you walk away; one walks away and all the squirrel can say is "Duh..."

What the little dim-witted acorn-eater doesn't know is that only one hunter walked away. So what happened to the other hunter? He is hunkering in ambush nearby. (Beginning to get the picture of where squirrel hunkering got its name, acorn-brain?) As the squirrel reappears and yells to his neighbor in the next tree, "Duh, ka-P-0-W." The hunter puts another one in the bag.

Now that the ban against goose creeping is on the books, I can already visualize how the regulations might read once the lawmakers zero in on squirrel hunkering..."It shall be unlawful to hunker within one hundred feet of a tree known to harbor a squirrel(s) for the express purpose of taking said squirrel or thereinafter causing such squirrel to be taken."

Can you imagine the shame, the humiliation, the embarrassment of having to face your wife and family should you be cited by the authorities for this crime against squirreldom? "Duh...hon, there's, er-ah, something I need to tell you," you'll stammer, hat in hand, eyes glued to the floor.

Sensing that trouble besets you and wanting to know she's on your side no matter what you've done, your wife and loving help-mate responds, "What have you gone and gotten yourself into this time, clabber-head?"

"I just got arrested by the game warden."

"What did you do this time?"

"Duh...I got caught squirrel hunkering."

"Whew...what a relief. I was afraid they'd caught you doing something really stupid. Like snipe sneaking."

A Shepherds Pie for Hunters

1 1/2	pounds ground venison
1	cup beef broth
1	teaspoon black pepper
2	bay leaves
2	whole cloves
1/4	teaspoon thyme leaves
1	cup diced carrots
1	cup sliced onion
2	cups sliced mushrooms
1	cup diced celery
1	cup whole kernel corn
1 1/2	tablespoons flour
1/2	cup red wine
1	pound cooked and diced potatoes
1	tablespoon butter
1/2	cup skim milk
1	tablespoon chopped chives
4	ounces mozzarella cheese

Brown meat in iron, or other, heavy skillet over medium flame. Drain in colander. Wipe skillet. Return meat to skillet and add the broth, pepper, bay leaves, cloves, and thyme. Cover skillet and simmer 30 minutes.

Add carrots, onion, mushrooms, celery and corn. Cover and allow to simmer until vegetables are tender. Lightly coat oven proof dish with oil. In small bowl, gradually add the wine to the flour, stirring to form a smooth paste. Add flour and wine paste to meat and vegetables. Simmer five minutes, until slightly thickened. Preheat oven to 375 degrees. Mash potatoes with butter, skim milk and chives. Place meat mixture on bottom of casserole dish, top with mashed potatoes and sprinkle the cheese over potato topping. Bake 10 minutes and serve hot. Serves 6.

Recipe by the American Heart Association

Louisiana Oyster Pie

2	pints oysters, small
1	bunch green onions, chopped
2	ribs celery, chopped
1	large white onion, chopped
4	cloves garlic finely chopped

Hot sauce to taste
Roux, dark brown, made from 3 tablespoons of flour and four tablespoon of oil
Unbaked pie shell and cover for 9-inch pie

Make a dark roux and set aside.

Chop vegetables. In separate skillet, saute vegetables in a small amount of vegetable oil until tender. Drain oysters and discard water.

In third skillet, bring oysters to a boil. Add sauted vegetables and the roux and hot sauce. When blended well, remove from heat. Pour into unbaked pie shell and cover with top crust. Make several slits into top. Bake in preheated 350 degree oven for approximately 30 minutes or until golden brown. Serves 6.

Recipe by the Times-Picayune